The Women Left Behind

Imogen Russell Williams

with illustrations by Chris Riddell

The Women Left Behind

© Imogen Russell Williams

Illustrations © Chris Riddell

Cover design: Nathan Brenville

First Edition 2019
ISBN: 978-1-907435-96-6

Imogen Russell Williams and Chris Riddell have asserted their authorship and given their permission to Dempsey & Windle for these poems and illustrations to be published here.

Published by Dempsey & Windle
15 Rosetrees
Guildford
Surrey
GU1 2HS
UK
01483 571164
dempseyandwindle.co.uk

A CIP record for this book can be obtained from the British Library.

'Now and then writer and subject are perfectly matched. This is true of Imogen Russell Williams and her stranded women, drawn from from mythology, drama, as well as adult and children's fiction. Each speaks out of her own situation - some bemused and seemingly helpless, some deeply distressed, some telling home truths about the shortcomings of men, some with a wonderful sense of the absurd, some exceedingly robust. Plenty of fine poets have written short monologues of this kind (among them Stevie Smith, Randall Jarrell, Leonard Cohen and Denise Levertov, Ted Hughes and Anne Sexton) - and now Russell Williams, pointing again and again to the sheer staying power of women, shows she has no less powerful an empathy, energy and good ear, and holds her own with them.'

Kevin Crossley-Holland

For Pererin and Devamonie, both of whom gave me poetry –
I will never leave you behind.

The Women Left Behind

One day I was thinking about the end of Henry James'
The Turn of the Screw – a governess cradling a dead
boy, trapped forever in ambiguous triumph – and
found myself suddenly desperate to know what
happened to the dead boy's sister, Flora. Miles and
Flora had shared so much throughout their strange and
eerie story; what would she do after her brother's
death, as a young woman from a wealthy background,
trailing secrets and scandal behind her like a shadow?

I tried to write a story about Flora, but the beginnings
of it became a poem instead. Then I began to see
short-changed, abandoned, stranded girls and women
in stories everywhere I looked, from the famous
figures of mythology to minor but significant
characters in plays, novels, operas and fairy-tales.
Pinned in perpetual limbo like insects in amber,
balked, denied, fobbed off or just forgotten, these left-
behind women filled me with a wish to write more
poems for them: little breath-bubbles where they
might speak (or scream) for themselves.

Imogen Russell Williams 2019

Contents

The Women Left Behind

ARIADNE

Ariadne
(Heroides)

I have been left
bereft
where the shale grits and the wave spits
derision.
Girl, you betrayed your
home on a whim,
a vision
of princely curls, Athenian
polish –
what price, now, the shambles-stinking
Labyrinth
where the jumbled bones of the best pubescents
lie,
like the driftwood
which I now collect for fire?

BET

Bet
(Oliver Twist)

Their bent backs are the worst. I don't know why.
You'd think it'd be booze – stale ale, jug-wine
 on stained, liverish mouths and heavy breaths –
or else their eyes, cracked egg-whites, crazed
with bloodworm threads, spilled tears of blue skim milk.
But no. Their backs, bent into burdened curves,
ox-broad, calf-stupid, with no byre's sweetness –
just ghostly weight they lade on, straight to me.
Pressed down, behind my eyes, I see her, too;
the bruises I laid cold pewter on,
a split lip, dabbled gently free of blood,
a torn hem, mended with a slapdash hand
as she did mine. My girl, the one
whose grimy paw sat delicate in mine
like smutted cambric. Skinny kids to spoiled mutton –
there was no hope for us. There never was,
but with you, dear, there was defiant joy,
flashing its ankles, over the abyss.

BLODEUWEDD

Blodeuwedd
(Mabinogion)

Owl flower owl owl flower. Who'd the right
To sweep up all my meadow-blooming dreams
And form me, petal softness, leaf-bone, vein,
Into a wifelike petrol-shop bouquet?
It galls, you know, to be so purpose-built,
A floral sex-toy, custom-made loophole
To sidle through, to plunge, a furrow plant,
And seed-child drive into my wild rich earth.
Dw i'n canu, but the words die on my tongue,
Curdled to screeches. I'd tell the truth again:
I wasn't made to be a hero's wife.

BRANWEN

8

Branwen
(Mabinogion)

My bright bird, sheen like petrol on the water
Broken in spangles by the roughened wave,
Speech-sweetened tongue, toes curling in my hair –
Fly, bird, and tell my brothers that my hands
Are rough as restless water. That my nails
Gnarl now like bird-feet, bitten down by lye.
Fly, bird, and tell my brothers that my tongue
That used to discourse music, has grown harsh
As ravens' with disuse – for none now speaks
To me, except with curses. If my child
Did not look up into my eyes, and smile,
And wrap his small fat arms about my neck
Breathing all sweetness, I'd long since have plunged
Into the petrol sea to try my wings,
Breaking my back to set my bird-soul free.

Fly, little bird, bearing my word of woe
And set the match to war, a whoomph of fuel
Like looking at the sun; and afterwards
A drift of blackened bones, all left to bob
On thoughtful, thoughtless, desultory waves
As though work, cruelty, bird had never been;
Marriage nor child, accord, discord,
Travel by ship or wing.

Your atom's weight sat lightly in my hand,
A spring compressed, a flame laid to a fuse.
Beyond my window, did the wild sea pause,
The spray held on the wind's breath, the wave's swell
Remaining pregnant with its own collapse?
And did the world wait, trapped in clear cement,
As long as it would take a breaking heart
To beat three times, before your body dipped,
Your wings spread like a handclap, and you flew?

DAPHNE

Daphne
(Metamorphoses)

You know my story, or you think you know –
how my dad snatched me from Apollo's touch
and left me reaching endlessly to heaven;

how my hair rippled and my fingers greened
and how within my blood cooled to slow sap,
my toes sinking through loam, learning contentment

of an arboreal kind, no longer chased, but chaste.

Well guess what chum, you don't know shit. I begged
to be rescued, not turned into a goddamn *tree*.
My would-be rapist wears my torn-off leaves.

That's not a happy ending.

EURYDICE

Eurydice
(Orpheus)

Here in the soft black ash I found some bone
in fragments: femur, little finger, rib
and strung together music of my own
for the first time.

Halt as a child's first footsteps, thud and plink,
a tonking tune like birdscratch on the air –
a blunt cascade, the overflowing brink
of a mud dam.

The music of my husband hales down suns.
He gets out his guitar, and plucks; extracts
with the strings' fall, the sweet note-runs,
his listeners' guts.

He had the heart from me. Of course he did –
when Orpheus plays for you, you will be played.
His lyre coiled me round. The serpent slid
up to my waist.

But now it seems I have come to prefer
my own halt limping music. With a chord
(strange, dissonant, dissolving in a blur)
I turn his head.

Flora
(The Turn of the Screw)

His watery reflection follows me,
Its rosebud-cruel mouth quirked with disdain
Or friendly satire. I sweep up my silken train,
And leave the window, tripping down to tea.
A hole remains where once I had a heart,
Filled with the brother who was all to me.
In our shared cryptic tongue, he calls to me,
Now, as, hair up, I try another start
In yet another place, pursued by eyes
And whispers, slanted smiles and secret-thieves.
Beloved footsteps scuttle through the leaves
Behind me; omens fleck the bird-rich skies.
I will not marry. To me clings a taint
That money cannot purge. I am alone
As if I were already dead. Yet one
Beguiling shade encircles me, restraint
And freedom in sweet-bitter warp and weft;
I am the living girl, the sister left.

HECUBA

Hecuba

(The Trojan Women, Hecuba)

I am not old
no matter what the silver water says
of silver hair
of silver scars   of wrinkles.

No, I am still the bride
brown-wristed, braid-looped, slim, whom Priam led
his shape blurred smoke-edged by the clinging veil –
his eyes, at last, so kind
seeing my fear.   Allaying it.

My fear was then of change
becoming that strange adult thing, a wife.
That fear surmounted, up then rose the fear
of barrenness –

then death, as howling freight
of baby freed himself
in great convulsive loops, garrotting pain.
Then babies' deaths. Then daughters lost to rape
and sons to violence.

That dream I had
of giving birth to firebrands and snakes –
that dream was one vague smudge
of terror in a life stretched taut by fear.
And I was right
to fear. Only my fear did not stretch far enough.

My Hector, doll, dragged empty in the dust
by a cruel child; my Priam, split and drained
like sacrifice, his body
left like meat.

My Deiphobus, Helenus, my girls –
Polyxena, bled dry on monster's tomb
Cassandra, giving tongue to her own death.
My city, scattered like a toddler's blocks
by smooth well-tended hands. I mourn
him too, my fatal son, the optimist. He wasn't built for war.

And my Astyanax, my grandson, best
whose eyebright smile creased plump brown cheeks
mere seconds after tears;
the dogs play spillikins with his ribs now, the birds
make nests of his fine hair.

I am not
the ancient lady standing in her rags
among her ruined greatness. I am not
the harpy with the blood under her nails who tore
and blinded, slew his sons who killed her child –
her littlest, latest child. I am not the queen
upon the dais, inclining my crowned head,
permitting them to take away my son
and leave him for the beasts. I am not old,
enslaved, bereaved, raising a snarl
in sudden dense-furred throat, a woman shaped
by fear and loss and vengeance to the form
of a bitch
safely entombed.

I am still
the girl, the girl, the girl with just one fear
half-longing, walking up with veil-blurred eyes
towards my destined outcome.

HETTY

18

Hetty
(The Picture of Dorian Gray)

I packed my toothpowder
and my best shawl,
trimmed with Grandma's birthday lace. I was

drunk
on the memory of our talk,
like wasps on jam
or rotten apples.

He made me laugh as all the flowers fell
into my hair, one by one, all my skin
burning
like long ago
when I tripped in the nettle-bed

And I saw myself
made May Queen in his eyes,
heavenly royal, just like he was in mine –
cream flannel untouched, no stain of the grass we lay on.

But alone
in the dawn's bitter brightness,
banishing night's shade
but not its chill,

I realised by degrees what he had seen:
my dress was dowdy,
and my tongue was tied.

HYRROKIN

Hyrrokin
(Gylfaginning)

Balder the beautiful, no surprise Hel opens for him
so willingly. I come for him,
the tears of Aesir and of every living thing
(almost)
dried
and I catch a little flicker of their sorrow –
but the one I feel sorry for? That one's
Hod.
It's no fun being peripheral,
perpetually endarkened, born the butt
of bearded jokes
behind
big, calloused hands –
but to be pulled into murder
by a yearning to belong –
well, I know a little about that, borne as I am
by wolves
restrained by snakes.

ISMENE

Ismene
(Antigone)

My sister, bird-boned, feather-light, iron-willed
Refused to let my brother lie and rot;
I always knew that it would get her killed.

I still remember how her feet were chilled
When she crept in beside me on the cot,
My sister, bird-boned, feather-light, iron-willed.

I knew at once the earth she must have spilled
Across his corpse, the undeserving sot.
I always knew that it would get her killed.

Sleep vanished, and my tired eyes filled
To think of her, a toy-spade-toting tot –
My sister, bird-boned, feather-light, iron-willed.

She could not leave *her* duty unfulfilled,
She told me, looking haughty – little snot.
I always knew that it would get her killed.

And now her quicksilver's forever stilled,
Her migratory feet bound to the spot.
My sister, bird-boned, feather-light, iron-willed –
I always knew that it would get her killed.

LOUISA

Louisa
(Hard Times)

Fire bursts out, father, when the evening comes,
when I sit celibate beside the hearth
consuming my own embers.

Fire bursts out through the dark untrodden cracks.
Behind the hanging and below the rug,
it smoulders, and remembers.

Fire bursts out when the evening draws the blinds.
A bitter blaze, contained by eyelids dropped,
and then expressed in scalding.

Fire falls in pinpricks on my faded knees,
my fingers raw, my nails severely short,
my knuckles white with holding.

I am an iron-boned furnace smelting hate
out of the jumbled ores of errors past.
Twice shattered and reforged, I hold my place

though not my peace: a fire-dog, singular;
Unbalanced, out of kilter, without ease
or purpose; broken, manifest disgrace.

My niche holds an enshrined statue Spite,
a static Fury with uplifted whip,
its bronze about to sing down on my self,

in place of more domestic gods. No warmth
but cold ice or cruel heat; no heaped-up cake
of offering; only dust upon the shelf.

LOUISE

26

Louise
(My Cousin Rachel)

That stupid boy. I don't blame her, you know –
or not as much as I once did. I blame
Saint Ambrose, dear dead dad could do no wrong,
who formed Phil in his image. Just the same
scorn of the 'female wish for constant talk';
insistence that the bachelor state was best,
shying from skirts, a startled white-eyed colt.
No need for mother hens in that stark nest –
just a lean, stringy, strutting dunghill cock,
showing his downy chick a hanging corpse
to season him. He seasoned him too well –
as the young sapling bends, the green tree warps.
Of course I loved him, stupid stuck-up fool
adoring at Ambrose's heels, a pup
not grown into his paws. But how could he,
gorging starved swallows from that sugared cup,
discern, untaught, the sting under the sweet?
He didn't know – until he came to know,
until he snuffed out her life, his – and mine,
all in a silent instant, undealt blow.
All promise broken, wasted, spilled and gone,
leaving a lingering breath of poison shame
to whisper in the air and cling to skin.
I'm glad the dead are there for me to blame.

MARGARET

Margaret
(Much Ado About Nothing)

Veiled I'll remain, a little stain of wine
faint, but that won't come out with scrubbing;
last year's model, just a tad shop-soiled
by time spent on display, there, in the window
sun-faded, mostly evenly; too brown
for daytime
but a bargain, if you don't look
at the new range, with its
crisp virginal lace;
one season only, everything must go

MARY

30

Mary
(Gulliver's Travels)

Oh, for fuck's sake, he's packed his trunk. What next?
He'll come back, raving, with some tiny sheep
or a giant needle, peering at his kids
and me as if we're somehow out of scale.
You know what? Wanderlust's a wondrous thing
when you can up and wander. When the soiled
and hungry, wailing, miscreant, unkempt
rely on you to feed, soothe, cleanse, chastise,
rising by night with clamour, splintering the days
of tedium with sharp intermittent fear –
Then you go sailing only deep within,
upon the surges of your beating blood,
wondering how the world can stretch so wide
for breech-clad thighs, while whalebone stays the women.
Just hold the small one, will you? I'm afraid
he's in the mews again, talking to the horses.

31

Mercédès

(The Count of Monte Cristo)

They came to my door so early,
calling me Catalane, beauty,
asking for cream and oranges
not two weeks after the wedding –

the wedding without a husband.
By inches I died, every hour;
as your dear father starved himself,
so love devoured me within.

Hollowed, I heard their voices
with ears like empty shells.
I took his succouring hand
With light dead dried-leaf fingers.

Then a new love: my son.

Impatient, indulged, adored,
my eye fed on his shadow.
I bear him in my blood still,
that blood you did not shed.

I consigned myself to the walls
where sorrow starved eating itself.
In gratitude for my child,
I undertook your imprisonment.

I did not grudge what is yours:
strange tastes, hummingbird colours,
smoke, sweetness, serried servants,
piled skins to step upon.

But we both bear time's predations,
each face tear-etched with acid.
My hair whitens; your aim falters.
We come from the same place.

I love you still. I still am lodged,
Sicilian grudge, beneath your ribs.
Forbear the seedling. Set youth free –
come lie, at ease, beneath the tree.

MERCÉDÈS

MICAËLA

Micaëla
(Carmen)

It leaves me doubled, dazed with childish coughing,
my first attempt to raise my darling's ghost
with breath, flame, cigarette.

But soon I learn to let the smoke curl out
like signals from dowsed beacons, dead but quick,
and there he stands again;

his chest still pushed out proud, through tattered silk
torn ragged-bright where emblems used to be…
Then, at his heels – she comes.

I know he murdered her. I'm not a fool.
I've seen a flash bird's neck wrung in my time.
(I've wrung a few myself.)

Both creatures always in him: sweet-faced lamb
and beer-roused bull, his tenderest touch
a grip that bruises wrists.

I'm taking off my apron, blue print gown,
letting my hair surge crackling from its plait.
I'm lighting up afresh

before I say goodbye to mother's grave,
pack – for myself, this time – a hearty meal
and take the road again.

PENELOPE

Penelope
(The Odyssey)

You know what I could burn? This fucking loom.
I've woven pious texts and sacred scenes
Until my fingers rage, my stooped neck smoulders.
Unpicking's almost worse – I can't just rip,
But have to ease the bastard shuttle back
In an erasing sweep, like the smooth smile
A wife assumes to greet her drunken man.
I've had it with the lot of them: the grins,
The smirking purr, hands cupped, to gauge my tits,
The braying satisfaction in my parlour.
Won't you come in, dear carrion-flies? I wish
That I were calm Athene, weaving war
And wrapping men in silken toils to smother;
Spider whose bite spells death, whose threads entrap.
She doesn't have to put up with this crap.

PHEBE

Phebe
(As You Like It)

It wasn't just the linens and the cloak.
(Though that fine work would pass a needle's eye,
that wool cost somebody her squinted sight
spinning by rushlight and by certain touch.)

It wasn't just the stinging flowers of speech
I gathered to my heart, although they blistered.
It wasn't that his barbed tongue stung my pride –
I don't want homage, and it makes me cruel.

No.
What I want: the slim form doubletted.
The bell-voiced tenor, not the deep-lunged bronze.
Cheek maiden-smooth that never will grow rough –
Sweet limbs that will not press or pin or pain.

And what I don't want –
why, a *good man's love*
And all the obligations in its train.

The pressing of the cheese, the spinning wool,
The bearing of his babes in blood and fear
With Death's head staring in the midwife's shade.

Down on your knees
And pray, weak woman, for a cleanly tomb.

Philotis
('Tis Pity She's a Whore)

My hands were always moved by others' hands,
Thin silk and ivory sticks to cast a shadow.
When needed, I could smile, pick out a tune;
Lay, upon eager skin, a breath-light kiss;
Alter my mind as I put off my gown;
Take up, obediently, the votive candle.

But, kindled now, an unaccustomed candle,
Held in my ribs' fortress, not by my hands,
Begins to burn beneath my novice gown
And cast a form unknown; a monstrous shadow
That lingers on the stone walls like the kiss
Of heavy smoke, dancing a devil's tune.

Never before now have I called the tune;
Sat late to study, and not saved the candle;
Or wondered what it might feel like to kiss
A man not wrought me by my uncle's hands.
Flitting about my cell like flesh made shadow,
My skin calls for another's through my gown.

Always I followed, whether doctor's gown
Or kinsman's cloak, keys ringing the same tune.
Always I have been another's shadow,
Erased at noon, seen only by the candle
Cupped in protective, secret, red-glow hands,
The click of teeth in lock my farewell kiss.

The rosary's dark beads click smooth, a kiss
To mitigate the harsh scratch of the gown
Wound tight about my frame, my nervous hands
Picking at threads, plucking a soundless tune.
I see it now – the game not worth the candle,
Wagering life as though it weighed a shadow.

40

I wish to be accounted more than shadow,
Than 'gentle', 'sweet', 'devoted'. Let me kiss
In the warm-ripened light of the sun's candle,
Wrapped in another's arms as in a gown –
I want clear birdsong for my mass's tune,
The mouth of love, not the confessor's hands.

It is too late to kiss. With his own hands
He laid the gown upon me, to the tune
Of silver, as the shadow snuffs the candle.

PHILOTIS

PIGGY'S
AUNTIE

42

Piggy's Auntie
(Lord of the Flies)

No, he didn't make friends easy,
did my nephew. Plump, you see –
a bit slow –

his breathing –
couldn't climb trees,
chase
run.

Clever, though –
grammar school. Very proud of him, we were
though the uniform
cost.
They teased him
cause he didn't
talk right
but he was
thick-skinned;
knew he'd show them
in the end.
But in the end, I suppose
they showed him.

ROSALINE

Rosaline
(Romeo and Juliet)

I took myself out of the marketplace;
laid my dancing shoes in lavender,
gave my quilted gowns and jewellery
to the girls who wanted rings.

Whispers of tragedy reached me
where I knelt to tell my beads –
then, briefly, I remembered
his hair's mulberry shine.

(I was young then myself,
But he will be young forever.)

For years I have been praying,
tending vines, thinning tomatoes,
teaching homesick neophytes
to sleep in cells of stone.

In sunlight laced with dust,
and root-smelling cold-damp cellars
I have breathed the air so long
that my lungs have learned its shape.

And the rictus of his death-mask
and the blood bloom on her shroud
have become light-faded frescos
whose colours do not hurt.

But every year they ripen,
those black and glossy berries,
and I wonder, for a moment,
would his hair have smelled so good?

SIGYN

Sigyn
(Gylfaginning)

And what would happen if I put it down,
this bowl of burning brew, and just – popped off?
Nipped to the corner-shop, ripped into a Twix
and kept on walking, sweetness in my teeth,
tossed pavement-wrapper skating at my heels?
What's here to keep me? Webs of wrought-iron grief,
anatomist's cat's cradle, gut-strung harp
playing one hoarse, diminished, red-eyed song –
the composition of one twisting pest,
one diseased vector, one ungodly god,
one cheating shithead husband. Toxic spume
of acid splashes, scarring up my wrist;
my fox-faced charmer, plunging in his bonds,
rucks up the earth like bedsheets. Well, my boy,
perhaps next time you'll listen when I say:
Don't kill him. Don't play false. Don't screw the gods
that one last fatal time, drunk on your cunning. You can hear
the drums' soft-mumbled thunder, spelling out
the syllables of doom. Take back your ball. Refuse to play.
Don't do it, though you can.

And should his anguish crack the great globe's crust,
if I laid down my chamber-pot and left
without my latch-key; well, too bad. So what.
I'm not afraid of earthquakes. I'm a god.
Besides, my fears
no matter how remote, have all come true.

THE 'HALF-CASTE'
WOMAN

The "Half-Caste" Woman
(Kim)

The serpent smoke rises upright
and spreads his hood, as though to fight,
while I crave, with strange phantom pain,
the presence of a child not mine.

Kutcha-butcha, half-baked bread
has no claim on the child she fed
clad in a brown that washes off.

I taught him what I knew of him –
to wear the clothes that I thought best;
to wear his past, an unseen charm,
in a sewn blessing on his breast –

I could not teach him of my love.

Sahib, my scholar, little, swift-tongued boy –
the doors stand wide for you, are shut to me.

THE PRINCESS

The Princess
(The Six Swans)

Hansie my favourite, he's the middle brother –
in six there is no middle. I made seven.
Gustav, Dolph, Friedrich, Hansie, Pieter, Will.
What burns more: nettle-hairs filled green with poison
swelling my finger-tips like blood balloons,
or the hot looks that dart my way from corners,
speaking condemning silence: "*Witchling…whore*"?
Three shirts are sewn now. Hansie, Pieter, Dolph –
Will's nose is always running, Friedrich farts,
and Gustav twists my arm. Sometimes I wish
that I was still an only-apple girl,
laid up in straw in my stone tower for storage.
The young king looks as well, stretching his neck
like cobs after the pen. His flat black eye
is colder than the pond's first fringe of ice
when winter breathes; and yet I feel it burn.

THE
SISTERS

The Sisters
(The Little Mermaid)

We cannot sit at leisure on our rocks
Combing the hair we sacrificed for you.
Our pelts are now seal-velvet, our wet eyes
Darkened with hurt, a stranger shade of blue.

Our tongues are sweet and salt, both hook and lure;
Our teeth are pearly still, though they've grown long.
The sailor churning water into cream
Drowns in a rockpool, drunk on our wild song.

We were laconic sea-girls, swirling tails
In sprays of light, scaled iridescent plunge.
Now beasts of prey, we cloud the limpid green
With sullied red, the deep lung-clawing lunge

And under. Death to he who stole you, sister,
And to his proxies – bifurcated things
As pale and fat as seaslugs. In your foam
They'll choke their last breath, while the selkie sings.

THE
SNOW QUEEN

The Snow Queen

Dissolving and reforming, in my veins
ice crackles, melts, speaks crystalline and sharp,
resonates
squeaks
whispers

                slips

and

shatters
into dust.
I set the puzzle that I sought to solve.
My cycle is disrupted. I reflect
a foreign body,
flesh and blood and salt.

Smart-arse, quick-talker;
facts curl off his tongue,
ice-calculations traced by bladed feet.

O fractal, brittle, little star
how I wonder   where you are?

Stellated polyhedron, porcupine
pierced/piercing, fragile mirror, glass-rod spine

child of my burning heart.

When he left here (with her) his new skates' knives
scored my blue-white permafrost
with the slash of a proven theorem.

THE WITCH

The Witch
(Rapunzel)

Rapunzel, Rapunzel, let your hair down, not your mother;
not she who bore you, knitting flesh from stolen salad,
but she who trained you upwards and preserved you from the blight
of uncouth eyes and greedy, grasping hands.
Out there a wasteland stretches,
filled with men who mount their conquests
as beasts their mates; no love, no secret knowledge,
only seed spilled, haste-hot, among the brambles.
Rapunzel, darling, O my climbing rose,
fed with my anxious hours, my old bones' dust –
do not grow crooked, or, parasite sprout,
send out the tiny shoots that spread to crack
the guardian stones, choke out the light, and smother
good counsel, gathered wisdom.
Let your hair down, not your mother.

THEA

Thea
(Hedda Gabler)

My head is heavy now. That weight of hair
She threatened to burn off – I'd lay it down
In sacrifice, if only I could sleep.

I've heard things, things I do not like to credit,
About his death, her gun, our paper child.
The daylight's coming makes me want to weep.

Another day in which the silence stretches,
Staining the hours like a teapot's sides.
I wouldn't mind, if only I could sleep.

Perhaps – if I lay down upon the sofa –
They'd disappear – the shrieking and the shot.
The circling sounds that make me want to weep.

I've disarranged my hair. What does it matter?
No, better to be seemly. There – my pins –
He liked it loose. If only I could sleep.

The servant clatters in the other room.
I wonder what she thinks. What do I think?
The thought of thinking makes me want to weep.

Under his hand my hair smoothed, and my tongue
Seemed to find sense, intelligence perhaps.
Our words could flow – if only I could sleep.

Why did she hate me so? And seem to pet me?
Demand I speak to her as 'du', a friend?
The image of her makes me want to weep.

I can see her, and him, hear shrieks and pistols,
Death, shame, demands, scorn, sweetness, love, contempt.
I think I could make sense if I could sleep.

THETIS

Thetis
(The Iliad)

My husband? Ash upon the wave,
Become invisible as salt,
For mortal years are very few
Though cities fall, and are despoiled.

I wanted something more for him,
The babe born of my changing shape,
The boy born of my change, by rape
From wild wave to child's rockpool.

But I did not have tongue to tell
That men's regard is shallow silt
And all that blood he shed and spilt
Would purchase only fame in Hell.

They say I destroyed all my sons
By fire, before Achilles came.
The truth is that I saved their lives
When I obscured and burned their names.

Tom
(Tom Tit Tot)

I never was the kind of heroine
apparently sustained by seed and dew:
bird-boned, earth-skimming, light as thistle-fluff,
clad in pure white, her long hair's gold fichu.
That's not me. I liked eating.
(I still do.)

Those pies my ma left cooling on the sill:
I liked the way my teeth met in the crust,
my jaws ached with the effort, four, five times.
 (Two mouthfuls each; I barely ate my fill.)

She called me lazy – well. True, I can't spin
(see here: my bloodied, blistered thumbs' reproof)
but split the timber wearing father's boots,
wielding his axe. Re-pitched the leaking roof,
drove nails – one clean iron-ringing stroke apiece –
plucked chickens bare, punched dough, heaved lumber home.

I take up space. I'm made of flesh.
My footsteps shake the ground I tread upon.

Lucky, I'm told
that he didn't ask for straw into gold;
only for flax to skeins, a woman's wealth.

Had he but looked
into my face, perhaps he would have seen
the kind of girl I was: the raucous health
drunk deep in beer to wash a long day down,
strong muscles trained to hold a half-shod horse,
spelling the smith; the long smirches of green
from hauling logs and dressing hafts, the skin
tanned brown, pale at the neck. I love the earth

that feeds me, sleeps me, bears me up, and takes
my mark as though it loves me in return.
I do not skim.
Or spin.

He did not look.

The year spins – I do not.
We have not much to talk about.
Until he spins, majestically, to show
a wheel, a cold-locked room, a plate of food
and flax on all sides,
lying in coils, like a good girl's hair.

Blood on the gold. A long-tailed visitation.
I make a promise I hope not to keep.

What's in a name? I try the ones I know.
I never thought of names that much before.

What is *my* name?

I never had a name pressed between pages,
preserving the faint scent of who I was. I am a *type*:
unstudied, greedy, imprudent; grasshopper
who plays away the summer
to wither with the frost.
Is my name Mary? May? Joanna?
Hope? Delilah? Jane?

I want a name
to wrap about my shoulders like a shawl –
Lanolin-rich, sheep-smelling, keep me dry.

I don't intend
to stay here, yearly purchasing my life
with mythic labour, growing with his child
and not my inclination.

I lick sauce from my knife. I swig, I burp,
and pour an ale libation.

Leaving the hanks of my unflaxen hair,
I will set forth new-named; taking *his* name,
the name of my deliverer that I stole,
the rights to myself with it. I belong
not to my mother, selling me for ease,
nor yet the king who would have butchered me,
nor to the eldritch atom who'd have freed
to chain me once again. I am my own

earth-shaking loud-voiced creature, breaking free
of rings and wheels, good wives and crowning glory.
Setting my teeth into my life's thick crust,
knowing my strength, I'll spin a single thread
in coarse bright ardent gold: tell my own story.

The Women Left Behind

Ariadne Daughter of King Minos of Crete, she falls in love with Theseus of Athens, giving him a ball of thread to guide him through her father's Labyrinth. As promised, Theseus takes her away with him, but then abandons her on the island of Naxos. (She is later discovered by Dionysus, god of wine, whom she marries.) Her complaint to Theseus appears in Ovid's *Heroides* (X).

Bet A minor character in Charles Dickens' *Oliver Twist* (1839), Bet is a close friend of Nancy's. Both women are 'free and easy in their manners', with 'a great deal of colour in their faces' – i.e., they're prostitutes – and both seem to have started out as child thieves for Fagin.

Blodeuwedd is a woman made of flowers by the magician Gwydion, from the collection of ancient Welsh tales called the *Mabinogion*. She is intended to be the wife of the hero Lleu Llaw Gyffes, who is cursed never to be able to marry a human woman – but when she falls in love with Gronw Pebr and conspires with him to murder Lleu, Gwydion turns her into an owl.

Branwen Another woman from the *Mabinogion*, Branwen is a Welsh princess given in marriage to Matholwych, King of Ireland. When her half-brother Efnisien mutilates her husband's horses, Branwen is held accountable; beaten and ill-treated, she tames a starling and sends it to tell her brother, King Bran the Blessed, of her humiliation. The resulting war wipes out almost the entire Welsh army, and the population of Ireland. Efnisien later burns Branwen's baby son.

Daphne A nymph, daughter of the river god Peneus. Pursued by lovestruck Apollo, she is changed by her father's power into a bay laurel tree; in her honour, Apollo always wears a wreath of laurel leaves afterwards. She appears in Ovid's *Metamorphoses* (I. 452-567).

Eurydice is the wife of Orpheus, who charms creatures and even stones with his music. When she is fatally bitten by a snake, Orpheus follows her to the Underworld, where Persephone and Hades agree that Eurydice may return to the land of the living, but only if Orpheus does not look back at her until they have both reached the surface. Orpheus looks round too early, condemning Eurydice to remain in the land of the dead. Virgil tells a version of the story in *Georgics IV*.

Flora In Henry James' 1898 novella *The Turn of the Screw*, eight-year-old Flora and her brother Miles seem to their new governess to be under the malign influence of two corrupt ghosts, Miss Jessel and Peter Quint. As fear and tension increase, Flora is taken away by Mrs Grose, the housekeeper, but ten-year-old Miles remains with the governess in their old home, and dies there.

Hecuba is the wife of King Priam of Troy, mother of Hector, Paris, Cassandra and many other children, several of whose deaths she witnesses. In Euripides' tragedy 'The Women of Troy', she recovers the body of her grandson Astyanax after he has been thrown from the walls of Troy. In 'Hecuba', she takes revenge on Polymestor, who killed her youngest son, by killing his own children and blinding him with her brooch. Some versions of her story say that she was turned into a dog and buried at the Dog's Tomb in the Hellespont.

Hetty Merton is a young village girl whom Oscar Wilde's Dorian Gray (*The Picture of Dorian Gray*, 1890) intends to seduce, then decides to leave unspoiled, hoping to prove to himself that he is still capable of virtue. They had agreed to run away together, but Dorian fails to keep their rendezvous.

Hyrrokin the giantess is called in by the gods of Asgard after the death of Balder, fairest of the gods, to drag his funeral ship Hringhorni out to sea, according to Snorri Sturluson's 13th century *Gylfaginning*. She arrives riding a giant wolf with vipers for reins.

Ismene is the older sister of *Antigone*, protagonist of Sophocles' tragedy of the same name. Unlike Antigone, Ismene obeys King Creon's edict that their brother Polyneices must be left unburied, frightened of what will happen if she disobeys. When Antigone buries Polyneices, Ismene tries to 'confess', but Antigone will not permit it – Ismene's life is spared, but Antigone is condemned to be buried alive.

Louisa Gradgrind, later Bounderby, in Dickens' *Hard Times* (1854), is the daughter of Thomas Gradgrind, brought up on Utilitarian principles and encouraged to value only facts, despising creativity and emotion. Her loveless marriage to Josiah Bounderby, to which she agrees for her brother's sake, breaks down when she is tempted to have an affair, leaving her desolate, with no second chance at marriage or domestic happiness.

Louise Kendall, in Daphne du Maurier's My Cousin Rachel (1951), is a close childhood friend of Philip Ashley, a young man brought up by his misogynist cousin Ambrose. When Ambrose unexpectedly marries, then dies not long after, Philip becomes infatuated with his charismatic widow Rachel, rejecting any criticism of her from Louise or others. Wavering between love and suspicion, Philip eventually causes Rachel's death by failing to warn her that the bridge in the garden is unsafe.

Margaret is Hero's waiting-gentlewoman in the Shakespearean comedy *Much Ado About Nothing*. Margaret inadvertently allows her mistress to be accused of unchastity when she is persuaded to appear at Hero's window by her lover Borachio, and lets him call her by Hero's name.

Mary Burton Gulliver is the wife of Lemuel Gulliver (*Gulliver's Travels* by Jonathan Swift, 1726), who presents her with several children between his voyages of exploration to Lilliput, Brobdingnag, Laputa and the land of the Houynhnhms.

Mercédès is the young fiancée of Edmond Dantès, later *The Count of Monte Cristo* (1844), hero of Alexandre Dumas' eponymous novel. On their wedding day, Dantès is falsely accused of treason; after many years' imprisonment, he escapes to discover that his father has died of starvation and Mercédès has married one of the men who conspired against him. Seeking revenge on his enemies, Dantès cannot bring himself to harm Mercédès or her son; however, he is now involved with a young Greek girl named Haydée.

Micaëla, in Georges Bizet's opera, is the antithesis of *Carmen* (1875). A village girl with hair in two long plaits, wearing a a demure blue frock and apron, Micaëla comes to Seville, contending with Carmen's fatal appeal, to try to bring her soldier beau Don José home to his mother.

Penelope, wife of Odysseus (*The Odyssey*), keeps her importunate suitors at bay while her husband makes his ten-year journey home from Troy by weaving by day and unravelling by night, promising to choose a new husband when her work is finished.

Philotis, the niece of Richardetto, is a minor character in John Ford's tragedy *'Tis Pity She's A Whore*, first performed in the 1620s. Disguised as a doctor, Richardetto is in Parma seeking revenge on Soranzo, the nobleman who cuckolded him. As the main plot unfolds in incest, murder and conspiracy, Philotis, posing as a musician, becomes betrothed at Richardetto's bidding to Bergetto, a rich but stupid young man; after her fiancé is stabbed to death, her uncle counsels her to enter a convent.

Phebe is a shepherdess who falls in love with Rosalind, heroine of Shakespeare's *As You Like It*, when Rosalind is disguised as the shepherd Ganymede. Rosalind tells her scornfully to be grateful for the love of Silvius, another shepherd, who is infatuated with her.

Piggy's Auntie In William Golding's *Lord of the Flies* (1954), Piggy's father is dead, and his mother is mysteriously absent; his auntie, who gives Piggy 'ever so many sweets' from the sweetshop she keeps, and won't let him run because of his asthma, is the person who has brought him up. (With thanks to William Golding Ltd, and Faber & Faber.)

Rosaline is the subject of Romeo's first infatuation in *Romeo and Juliet*. Though Romeo bemoans the fact that she has sworn to remain chaste, his hope of seeing her spurs him to gate-crash the Capulet party where he first meets Juliet.

Sigyn, a goddess herself, is the long-suffering wife of the trickster Loki. In *Gylfaginning*, when the gods of Asgard punish Loki for the death of Balder by binding him (with his son's guts) under the venom-dripping fangs of a great serpent, Sigyn holds a bowl to keep the poison from Loki's face. Loki's anguish, when she takes away and empties the bowl, is said to be the cause of earthquakes which hasten the day of Ragnarok.

The "Half-Caste" Woman takes care of Rudyard Kipling's *Kim* (1901) at the beginning of the book, before he abandons her to set out on the 'Great Game' of espionage. She encourages him to wear Western clothes and the papers that prove his identity, which she has sewn into a charm for him to wear round his neck.

The Princess in *The Six Swans*, from *Children's and Household Tales* by the Brothers Grimm (1812), is the youngest child of a king who has married again. Her stepmother, skilled in witchcraft, curses her six brothers to take the form of swans; the Princess can only save them by sewing six shirts out of nettles, and by staying silent for six years. Sewing the shirts in the forest, she is discovered by another king, who brings her to his court; he marries her, but his mother takes advantage of her silence to accuse her of witchcraft and child-murder. There are many variations on this story.

The Sisters of Hans Christian Andersen's *Little Mermaid* (1837) give their hair to the Sea Witch in return for an enchanted knife. If the Little Mermaid, now voiceless and in human form after falling in love with a mortal Prince, can stab him with it, she will save her own life; otherwise she will turn to sea-foam.

The Snow Queen, also from a story by Hans Christian Andersen (1844), is Queen of the snow bees (snowflakes). Promising the world and a new pair of skates, she tempts Kay, a boy made cold and calculating by splinters of the Devil's broken mirror lodged in his eye and heart, to leave his home and come to live in her palace. Gerda, Kay's dearest friend, sets out to rescue him, and finds him trapped on a frozen lake called the Mirror of Reason, trying to spell 'Eternity' in ice.

The Witch keeps a young girl called *Rapunzel* (Grimm, 1812), named for the leaf her mother craves in pregnancy and sends her husband to steal from the Witch's garden, imprisoned in a high tower. In earlier versions of the story, the Witch expels Rapunzel from the tower when she discovers her pregnancy.

Thea Elvsted, an old school-mate of *Hedda Gabler* (Henrik Ibsen, 1891), abandons her husband and family to follow Ejlert Lövborg, scholar and alcoholic, whose muse she is and with whom she has fallen in love. Hedda's jealousy, and her wish to eliminate Ejlert as a rival to her own husband, prompts her to drive Ejlert to suicide.

Thetis, mother of Achilles, is a Nereid sea-goddess with the power to change her shape. It was prophesied that Thetis' son would be greater than his father, so Zeus and Poseidon, who had both desired her, decided that she should be married – against her will – to the mortal king Peleus. Some stories say that she had seven children, all of whom she killed in the attempt to make them immortal. In the *Iliad*, she comforts Achilles after Patroclus' death, and asks Hephaestus to forge him new armour to replace what he has lost.

Tom Tit Tot is an English version of *Rumpelstiltskin*, in which a woman sings ruefully that her daughter has eaten five pies. When the King overhears, the mother, ashamed, changes the song to 'spun five skeins today'. Struck by such industry, the King agrees to marry the daughter if, for one month out of every year, she will spin five skeins daily; if not, he will kill her. A little long-tailed 'impet' appears to help the daughter, but if she does not guess his name – Tom Tit Tot – by the end of the month, she will belong to him.